Bacon
COOKBOOK

Publications International, Ltd.

Some of the products listed in this publication may be in limited distribution.

Front cover photography and photography on pages 5, 15, 23, 35, 43, 49, 55, 65, 73, 79, 83, 93, 101, 115, 117, 125, 127, 133 and 135 by PIL Photo Studio.
Photographer: Tate Hunt
Photographer's Assistant: Tony Favarula, Justin Paris
Food Stylists: Kim Hartman, Rick Longhi
Assistant Food Stylist: Michael Deuson, Sheila Grannen
Prop Stylist: Tom Hamilton

Pictured on the front cover: Chicken, Bacon and Vegetable Sandwiches (*page 66*).
Pictured on the back cover *(clockwise from top):* Grilled Chicken Sandwiches with Basil Spread with Real Mayonnaise (*page 82*), Simmered Split Pea Soup (*page 64*), Chicken and Bacon Skewers (*page 100*) and Cheesy Scramblin' Pizza (*page 22*).

ISBN-13: 978-1-60553-710-8
ISBN-10: 1-60553-710-1

Library of Congress Control Number: 2010926310

Manufactured in China.

8 7 6 5 4 3 2 1

Microwave Cooking: Microwave ovens vary in wattage. Use the cooking times as guidelines and check for doneness before adding more time.

Preparation/Cooking Times: Preparation times are based on the approximate amount of time required to assemble the recipe before cooking, baking, chilling or serving. These times include preparation steps such as measuring, chopping and mixing. The fact that some preparations and cooking can be done simultaneously is taken into account. Preparation of optional ingredients and serving suggestions is not included.

pil

Publications International, Ltd.

CONTENTS

WAKIN' UP
WITH BACON

Bacon & Potato Frittata

3 tablespoons butter or margarine
2 cups frozen O'Brien hash brown potatoes
   with onions and peppers
5 eggs
½ cup bacon, crisp-cooked and crumbled
¼ cup half-and-half or milk
⅛ teaspoon salt
⅛ teaspoon black pepper

1. Preheat broiler.

2. Melt butter in large ovenproof skillet over medium-high heat. Swirl butter up side of pan to prevent eggs from sticking. Add potatoes; cook 4 minutes, stirring occasionally.

3. Beat eggs in medium bowl. Add bacon, half-and-half, salt and pepper; mix well. Pour egg mixture into skillet; reduce heat to medium. Cover and cook 6 minutes or until eggs are set at edges (top will still be wet).

4. Transfer skillet to broiler. Broil 4 inches from heat 1 to 2 minutes or until golden brown and center is set. Cut into wedges.   *Makes 4 to 6 servings*

Serving Suggestion: Top frittata with red bell pepper strips, chopped chives and salsa.

Prep and Cook Time: 20 minutes

Breakfast Empanadas

1 package (15 ounces) refrigerated pie crusts, cut into halves to make 4 semicircles

9 eggs, divided

1 teaspoon water

1 teaspoon salt

Dash black pepper

1 tablespoon butter

½ pound bacon (about 10 slices), crisp-cooked and cut into ¼-inch pieces

2 cups (8 ounces) Mexican-style shredded cheese, divided

4 tablespoons salsa

1. Preheat oven to 425°F. Spray baking sheet with nonstick cooking spray. Place pie crusts on prepared baking sheet.

2. Beat 1 egg and water in small bowl until well blended; set aside. Beat remaining 8 eggs, salt and pepper in medium bowl until well blended. Heat large skillet over medium heat. Add butter; tilt skillet to coat bottom. Sprinkle bacon evenly in skillet. Pour eggs into skillet and cook 2 minutes without stirring. Gently start stirring until eggs form large curds and are still slightly moist. Transfer to plate to cool.

3. Spoon one fourth of cooled scrambled egg mixture onto half of each pie crust. Reserve ¼ cup cheese; sprinkle remaining cheese evenly over eggs. Top with salsa.

4. Brush inside edges of each semicircle with reserved egg-water mixture. Fold dough over top of egg mixture and seal edges with fork. (Flour fork tines to prevent sticking, if necessary.) Brush tops of empanadas with remaining egg-water mixture and sprinkle with reserved ¼ cup cheese.

5. Bake 15 to 20 minutes or until golden.   *Makes 4 servings*

Cheesy Quichettes

12 slices bacon, crisp-cooked and chopped
 6 eggs, beaten
 ¼ cup whole milk
1½ cups refrigerated shredded hash brown potatoes
 ¼ cup chopped fresh parsley
 ½ teaspoon salt
1½ cups (6 ounces) shredded Mexican cheese blend with jalapeño peppers

1. Preheat oven to 400°F. Lightly spray 12 standard (2½-inch) muffin cups with nonstick cooking spray.

2. Place equal amounts of bacon into prepared muffin cups. Beat eggs and milk in medium bowl. Add potatoes, parsley and salt; mix well. Spoon mixture evenly into muffin cups.

3. Bake 15 minutes or until knife inserted into centers comes out almost clean. Sprinkle with cheese; let stand 3 minutes or until cheese melts. (Egg mixture will continue to cook while standing.*) To remove from pan, gently run knife around outer edges and lift out with fork.

Makes 12 quichettes

*Standing also allows for easier removal of quichettes from pan.

California Croissants

1 teaspoon vinegar*
4 eggs
2 croissants, halved and toasted
4 slices tomato
½ avocado, sliced crosswise
8 slices bacon, crisp-cooked
Mornay Sauce (recipe follows)
Chopped chives and alfalfa sprouts

Adding vinegar to the water helps keep the egg white intact while poaching.

1. Fill wide deep skillet with about 1½ inches water; add vinegar. Bring to a simmer. Break 1 egg into shallow cup or saucer; gently slide egg into skillet. Repeat with remaining eggs.

2. Cook eggs 3 to 4 minutes or until set. Carefully remove eggs with slotted spoon; drain on paper towels.

3. Place croissant half on each plate. Layer tomato, avocado and bacon on croissants. Top with eggs. Divide Mornay Sauce equally among croissants. Garnish with chives and sprouts. *Makes 4 servings*

Mornay Sauce

2 tablespoons butter or margarine
2 tablespoons all-purpose flour
1½ cups milk
¼ cup (1 ounce) shredded Cheddar cheese
2 tablespoons grated Parmesan cheese
½ teaspoon Dijon-style mustard
¼ teaspoon salt
⅛ teaspoon white pepper

1. Melt butter in medium saucepan over medium heat. Add flour; stir until bubbly.

2. Gradually stir in milk; cook until mixture comes to a boil and thickens, stirring constantly.

3. Stir in cheeses, mustard, salt and pepper. Remove from heat; stir until cheese is melted. *Makes about 1¾ cups*

California Croissant

Bacon-Cheddar Muffins

2 cups all-purpose flour
¾ cup sugar
2 teaspoons baking powder
½ teaspoon baking soda
½ teaspoon salt
¾ cup plus 2 tablespoons milk
⅓ cup butter, melted and cooled
1 egg
1 cup (4 ounces) shredded Cheddar cheese
6 slices bacon, crisp-cooked and crumbled

1. Preheat oven to 350°F. Grease 12 standard (2½-inch) muffin cups.

2. Combine flour, sugar, baking powder, baking soda and salt in medium bowl. Combine milk, butter and egg in small bowl; mix well. Add milk mixture to flour mixture; stir just until blended. Gently stir in cheese and bacon. Spoon batter into prepared muffin cups, filling three-fourths full.

3. Bake 15 to 20 minutes or until toothpick inserted into centers comes out clean. Cool in pan 2 minutes; remove to wire rack. Serve warm or at room temperature.   *Makes 12 muffins*

BACON BITS

When making muffins, don't grease any cups that won't be filled since the fat will burn and make your pan hard to clean. Instead, add two or three tablespoons of water to any empty cups to keep the pan from heating unevenly and/or warping in the oven.

Caramelized Bacon

12 slices (12 ounces) applewood-smoked bacon
½ cup packed light brown sugar
2 tablespoons water
¼ to ½ teaspoon ground red pepper

1. Preheat oven to 375°F. Line 15×10-inch jelly-roll pan with heavy-duty foil. Spray wire rack with nonstick cooking spray; place in prepared pan.

2. Cut bacon in half crosswise; arrange in single layer on prepared wire rack. Combine sugar, water and red pepper in small bowl; mix well. Brush generously over surface of bacon.

3. Bake 20 to 25 minutes or until bacon is dark brown. Immediately transfer to serving platter; cool completely.   *Makes 6 servings*

Note: Bacon can be prepared up to 3 days ahead and stored in the refrigerator between sheets of waxed paper in a large resealable food storage bag. Let stand at room temperature at least 30 minutes before serving.

Buckwheat Browns

1 cup cooked soba noodles, drained and chopped well
⅓ cup bacon, crisp-cooked and chopped
⅓ cup minced parsley
¼ cup minced red bell pepper
1 teaspoon minced garlic
1 egg white, beaten until foamy
½ teaspoon black pepper
Nonstick cooking spray

1. Mix noodles with bacon, parsley, bell pepper, garlic, egg white and black pepper; stir well. (Egg white should be partially absorbed.)

2. Spray large skillet with cooking spray; heat over medium-high heat. Use ¼ cup measure to scoop noodle mixture onto skillet. Cook 3 to 4 minutes. Spray each noodle cluster with cooking spray; turn and cook 3 to 4 minutes or until noodles are browned at edges. Serve warm.
Makes 6 servings

Bacon and Cheese Brunch Potatoes

3 medium russet potatoes, peeled and cut into 1-inch pieces
1 cup chopped onion
½ teaspoon seasoned salt
4 slices bacon, crisp-cooked and crumbled
1 cup (4 ounces) shredded sharp Cheddar cheese
1 tablespoon chicken broth or water

SLOW COOKER DIRECTIONS

1. Coat slow cooker with nonstick cooking spray. Layer half of potatoes, onion, seasoned salt, bacon and cheese in slow cooker. Repeat layers, ending with cheese. Pour broth over top.

2. Cover; cook on LOW 6 hours or on HIGH 3½ hours. Stir gently to mix and serve hot. *Makes 6 servings*

Cheese Grits with Chiles and Bacon

6 slices bacon, divided
1 jalapeño pepper, minced
1 large shallot or small onion, finely chopped
4 cups chicken broth
1 cup uncooked grits
¼ teaspoon black pepper
   Salt
1 cup (4 ounces) shredded Cheddar cheese
½ cup half-and-half
2 tablespoons finely chopped green onion

SLOW COOKER DIRECTIONS

1. Cook bacon in medium skillet until crisp. Drain on paper towels. Crumble 2 slices into slow cooker. Refrigerate remaining bacon.

2. Drain all but 1 tablespoon bacon drippings from skillet. Add jalapeño pepper and shallot. Cook and stir over medium-high heat 1 minute or until shallot is lightly browned. Transfer to slow cooker. Stir broth, grits, black pepper and salt into slow cooker. Cover; cook on LOW 4 hours.

3. Stir in cheese and half-and-half. Sprinkle with green onion. Crumble reserved bacon over grits. *Makes 4 servings*

Bacon and Cheese Brunch Potatoes

Quick Bacon & "Egg-Wich"

WHAT YOU NEED

1 whole wheat English muffin, split
1 egg
1 thin slice tomato
1 slice OSCAR MAYER® Fully Cooked Bacon, cut in half
1 slice (½ ounce) VELVEETA® 2% Milk Pasteurized Prepared Cheese Product

MAKE IT

1. PLACE 1 English muffin half on microwavable plate. Carefully crack egg over muffin. Microwave on HIGH 40 seconds.

2. TOP with tomato, bacon and VELVEETA®; cover with remaining muffin half.

3. MICROWAVE on HIGH 30 seconds or until egg white is completely set and yolk is thickened around the edge.   *Makes 1 serving*

Prep Time: 1 minute
Total Time: 2 minutes 10 seconds

BACON BITS

Enjoy this hot sandwich as a quick grab-'n'-go breakfast.
Simply wrap it in foil before heading out the door.

Bacon and Egg Cups

12 slices bacon, crisp-cooked and cut crosswise into thirds
6 eggs
½ cup diced bell pepper
½ cup shredded pepper jack cheese
½ cup half-and-half
¼ teaspoon salt
¼ teaspoon black pepper

1. Preheat oven to 350°F. Lightly spray 12 standard (2½-inch) muffin cups with nonstick cooking spray.

2. Place 3 bacon slices in each prepared muffin cup, overlapping in bottom. Beat eggs, bell pepper, cheese, half-and-half, salt and black pepper in medium bowl until well blended. Fill each muffin cup with ¼ cup egg mixture.

3. Bake 20 to 25 minutes or until eggs are set in center. Run knife around edge of each cup before removing from pan.

Makes 12 servings

Tip: To save time, look for mixed diced bell peppers in the produce section of the grocery store.

Cheesy Scramblin' Pizza

WHAT YOU NEED

6 eggs
¼ cup milk
¼ cup sliced green onions
1 small tomato, chopped
1 Italian pizza crust (12 inch)
½ pound (8 ounces) VELVEETA® Pasteurized Prepared Cheese Product, cut into ½-inch cubes
6 slices OSCAR MAYER® Ready to Serve Bacon, cut into 1-inch pieces

MAKE IT

1. PREHEAT oven to 450°F. Beat eggs, milk, onions and tomato with wire whisk until well blended. Pour into medium skillet sprayed with nonstick cooking spray. Cook on medium-low heat until eggs are set, stirring occasionally.

2. PLACE pizza crust on baking sheet; top with egg mixture and VELVEETA®. Sprinkle with bacon.

3. BAKE 10 minutes or until VELVEETA® is melted. Cut into wedges to serve.   *Makes 8 servings, 1 wedge each*

Substitute: Substitute ½ pound (8 ounces) VELVEETA® Mild Mexican Pasteurized Prepared Cheese Product with Jalapeño Peppers for the VELVEETA® Pasteurized Prepared Cheese Product.

Prep Time: 10 minutes
Bake Time: 10 minutes

Easy Cheesy Bacon Bread

1 pound sliced bacon, chopped
1 large onion, chopped
1 large green bell pepper, chopped
½ teaspoon ground red pepper
3 cans (7½ ounces each) refrigerated buttermilk biscuits, quartered
2½ cups (10 ounces) shredded Cheddar cheese, divided
½ cup (1 stick) butter, melted

1. Preheat oven to 350°F. Spray nonstick bundt pan with nonstick cooking spray.

2. Cook bacon in large skillet over medium heat about 4 minutes or until crisp. Drain on paper towels. Reserve 1 tablespoon drippings in skillet. Add onion, bell pepper and red pepper; cook and stir over medium-high heat about 10 minutes or until tender. Cool.

3. Combine biscuit pieces, bacon, onion mixture, 2 cups cheese and melted butter in large bowl; mix gently. Loosely press mixture into prepared pan.

4. Bake 30 minutes or until golden brown. Cool 5 minutes in pan on wire rack. Invert onto serving platter and sprinkle with remaining ½ cup cheese. Serve warm. *Makes 12 servings*

Spinach Sensation

1 cup sour cream
3 eggs, separated
2 tablespoons all-purpose flour
⅛ teaspoon black pepper
1 package (10 ounces) frozen chopped spinach, thawed and squeezed dry
½ cup (2 ounces) shredded sharp Cheddar cheese
½ pound bacon slices, crisp-cooked and crumbled
½ cup plain dry bread crumbs
1 tablespoon butter, melted

1. Preheat oven to 350°F. Lightly coat 2-quart round baking dish with nonstick cooking spray.

2. Whisk sour cream, egg yolks, flour and pepper in large bowl until blended. Beat egg whites in medium bowl with electric mixer at high speed until stiff peaks form. Stir one fourth of egg whites into sour cream mixture; fold in remaining egg whites.

3. Arrange half of spinach in prepared baking dish. Top with half of sour cream mixture. Sprinkle with ¼ cup cheese. Top evenly with bacon. Repeat layers, ending with cheese.

4. Combine bread crumbs and butter in small bowl; sprinkle evenly over top. Bake 30 to 35 minutes or until center is set. Let stand 5 minutes before serving.   *Makes 6 servings*

Bacon and Eggs Brunch Casserole

1 tube (8 ounces) refrigerated crescent roll dough
6 eggs
½ cup milk
1 cup (4 ounces) SARGENTO® Chef Style Shredded Mild
  Cheddar Cheese
8 slices bacon, diced and cooked crisp

SPRAY a 13×9-inch baking pan with non-stick cooking spray. Unroll dough and press into bottom of pan. Bake in preheated 350°F oven 10 minutes.

BEAT together eggs and milk in medium bowl. Pour over partially baked dough. Sprinkle with cheese and bacon; return to oven and bake 25 minutes more or until center is set. *Makes 6 servings*

Prep Time: 15 minutes
Cook Time: 35 minutes

Swiss Onion Potatoes Rosti

1 tablespoon olive oil
½ cup crumbled cooked bacon
5 cups shredded fresh or frozen potatoes
1⅓ cups *French's*® French Fried Onions
1 cup (4 ounces) shredded Swiss or Cheddar cheese
  Applesauce or sour cream (optional)

1. Heat oil in 10-inch nonstick skillet over medium-high heat. Cook bacon 1 minute. Stir in potatoes, French Fried Onions and cheese. Cook 8 minutes or until lightly browned on bottom.

2. Loosen mixture and gently invert onto large serving platter. Return to skillet and cook 6 minutes or until browned.

3. Remove to serving platter. Season to taste with salt and pepper. If desired, serve with dollop of applesauce or sour cream on the side.

Makes 4 to 6 servings

Prep Time: 5 minutes
Cook Time: 15 minutes

APPETIZERS GONE HOG WILD

Cream Cheese Bacon Crescents

WHAT YOU NEED

- **1 package (8 ounces) PHILADELPHIA® Cream Cheese, softened**
- **8 slices OSCAR MAYER® Bacon, crisply cooked, crumbled**
- **⅓ cup KRAFT® 100% Grated Parmesan Cheese**
- **¼ cup finely chopped onion**
- **2 tablespoons chopped fresh parsley**
- **1 tablespoon milk**
- **2 cans (8 ounces each) refrigerated crescent dinner rolls**

MAKE IT

1. PREHEAT oven to 375°F. Mix cream cheese, bacon, Parmesan cheese, onion, parsley and milk until well blended; set aside.

2. SEPARATE each can of dough into 8 triangles. Spread each triangle with 1 rounded tablespoonful of cream cheese mixture. Cut each triangle lengthwise into 3 narrow triangles. Roll up, starting at wide ends. Place point-side down on greased baking sheet.

3. BAKE 12 to 15 minutes or until golden brown. Serve warm.

Makes 4 dozen or 24 servings, 2 crescents each

Jazz It Up: Sprinkle lightly with poppy seeds before baking.

Prep Time: 30 minutes
Bake Time: 15 minutes

Bacon-Wrapped BBQ Chicken

8 chicken tenders (about 1 pound)
½ teaspoon paprika or cumin (optional)
8 slices bacon
½ cup barbecue sauce, divided

1. Preheat broiler. Line broiler pan with foil.

2. Sprinkle chicken tenders with paprika, if desired. Wrap each chicken tender with slice of bacon in spiral pattern; place on prepared pan.

3. Broil chicken 4 minutes. Turn and broil 2 minutes. Brush with ¼ cup barbecue sauce; broil 2 minutes. Turn and brush with remaining ¼ cup barbecue sauce; broil 2 minutes or until chicken is no longer pink in center.

Makes 4 servings

Festive Bacon & Cheese Dip

2 packages (8 ounces each) cream cheese, cut into cubes
4 cups (16 ounces) shredded Colby-Jack cheese
1 cup half-and-half
2 tablespoons prepared mustard
1 tablespoon minced onion
2 teaspoons Worcestershire sauce
½ teaspoon salt
¼ teaspoon hot pepper sauce
1 pound bacon, crisp-cooked and crumbled
Crusty bread and vegetables (optional)

SLOW COOKER DIRECTIONS

1. Combine cream cheese, Colby-Jack cheese, half-and-half, mustard, onion, Worcestershire sauce, salt and pepper sauce in 1½-quart slow cooker.

2. Cover; cook on LOW 1 hour or until cheese melts, stirring occasionally.

3. Stir in bacon; adjust seasonings. Serve with crusty bread or vegetable dippers.

Makes about 4 cups dip

Ranch-Style Shrimp and Bacon Appetizers

Ranch-Style Barbecue Sauce (recipe follows)
30 large peeled, deveined shrimp
½ pound thick-cut bacon
10 wooden skewers*

To prevent wooden skewers from burning while grilling or broiling, soak in water about 10 minutes before using.

1. Prepare Ranch-Style Barbecue Sauce.

2. Wrap each shrimp with ½ bacon strip. Thread 3 wrapped shrimp onto each wooden skewer.

3. Grill or broil shrimp skewers until bacon is cooked and shrimp is no longer translucent, but has turned pink. Baste with Barbecue Sauce. Return to heat to warm sauce. Serve with additional Barbecue Sauce, if desired. *Makes 10 shrimp skewers*

Ranch-Style Barbecue Sauce

¼ cup vegetable or olive oil
½ cup minced onion
2 garlic cloves, minced
2 tablespoons lemon juice
1 tablespoon ground black pepper
1 teaspoon *each* dry mustard and paprika
½ teaspoon *each* salt and hot pepper sauce
1½ cups ketchup
1 cup HEATH® BITS 'O BRICKLE® Toffee Bits
¼ cup cider vinegar
3 tablespoons sugar
1½ tablespoons HERSHEY®S Cocoa

1. Heat oil in large saucepan over medium heat; add onion and garlic. Cook until tender. Stir in lemon juice, black pepper, mustard, paprika, salt and hot pepper sauce. Simmer for 5 minutes; reduce heat.

2. Stir in ketchup, toffee bits, vinegar, sugar and cocoa. Simmer 15 minutes. Refrigerate leftovers. *Makes 3 cups*

BLT Cukes

½ cup finely chopped lettuce
½ cup finely chopped baby spinach
3 slices bacon, crisp-cooked and crumbled
¼ cup finely diced tomato
1 tablespoon plus 1½ teaspoons mayonnaise
¼ teaspoon black pepper
⅛ teaspoon salt
1 large cucumber
Minced fresh parsley or green onion (optional)

1. Combine lettuce, spinach, bacon, tomato, mayonnaise, pepper and salt in medium bowl; mix well.

2. Peel cucumber; trim off ends and cut in half lengthwise. Use spoon to scoop out seeds; discard seeds.

3. Divide bacon mixture between cucumber halves, mounding in center. Garnish with parsley. Cut into 2-inch pieces. *Makes 8 to 10 pieces*

Barbecue Bacon Party Spread

WHAT YOU NEED

2 packages (8 ounces each) PHILADELPHIA® Cream Cheese, softened
½ cup KRAFT THICK 'N SPICY® Original Barbecue Sauce
1 package (2.8 ounces) OSCAR MAYER® Real Bacon Recipe Pieces
1 small tomato, chopped
½ cup chopped green bell pepper
⅓ cup sliced green onions
1½ cups KRAFT® Shredded Cheddar Cheese
TRISCUIT® Thin Crisps

MAKE IT

1. SPREAD cream cheese on large platter; drizzle with barbecue sauce.

2. TOP with all remaining ingredients except the Thin Crisps.

3. SERVE with the Thin Crisps. *Makes 35 servings*

Prep Time: 15 minutes

Bacon-Wrapped Fingerling Potatoes with Thyme

1 pound fingerling potatoes
2 tablespoons olive oil
1 tablespoon minced fresh thyme, plus additional for garnish
½ teaspoon black pepper
¼ teaspoon paprika
½ pound bacon slices
¼ cup chicken broth

SLOW COOKER DIRECTIONS

1. Toss potatoes with oil, thyme, pepper and paprika in large bowl.

2. Cut each bacon slice in half lengthwise; wrap half slice bacon tightly around each potato.

3. Heat large skillet over medium heat; add potatoes. Reduce heat to medium-low; cook until lightly browned and bacon has tightened around potatoes.

4. Place potatoes in 4½-quart slow cooker. Add broth. Cover; cook on HIGH 3 hours. Garnish with additional thyme.   *Makes 4 to 6 servings*

Prep Time: 45 minutes
Cook Time: 3 hours

 **BACON BITS**

This appetizer can be made even more eye-catching with rare varieties of potatoes. Many interesting varieties can be found at farmers' markets. Purple potatoes, about the size of fingerling potatoes, can add more color to this dish.

Smoky Bacon Mushroom Toasts

10 slices bacon
 1 onion, diced
 1 red bell pepper, diced
 2 packages (8 ounces each) mushrooms, diced
  Salt and black pepper
24 (½-inch) toasted French bread slices
  Chopped fresh parsley

1. Cook bacon in large skillet over medium heat until crisp. Drain on paper towels. Drain all but 2 tablespoons drippings from skillet.

2. Add onion and bell pepper to skillet; cook and stir over medium-high heat 2 minutes or until onions are tender. Add mushrooms; season with salt and black pepper. Cook and stir 8 to 10 minutes or until mushroom liquid is almost evaporated. Cool 5 minutes.

3. Crumble bacon. Spread 1½ tablespoons mushroom mixture on each bread slice. Sprinkle with crumbled bacon and parsley.

Makes 24 appetizers

BLT Dip

1 envelope LIPTON® RECIPE SECRETS® Onion Soup Mix*
 1 container (8 ounces) sour cream
 1 cup HELLMANN'S® or BEST FOODS® Real Mayonnaise
 1 medium tomato, chopped (about 1 cup)
 ½ cup cooked crumbled bacon (about 6 slices) or bacon bits
  Shredded lettuce

*Also terrific with LIPTON® RECIPE SECRETS® Golden Onion Soup Mix.

1. In medium bowl, combine all ingredients except lettuce; chill, if desired.

2. Garnish with lettuce and serve with your favorite dippers.

Makes 3 cups dip

Prep Time: 10 minutes

Cheese & Bacon Jalapeño Rellenos

WHAT YOU NEED

4 ounces (½ of 8-ounce package) PHILADELPHIA® Cream Cheese, softened

1 cup KRAFT® Shredded Cheddar Cheese

4 slices OSCAR MAYER® Bacon, cooked, crumbled

2 tablespoons finely chopped onions

2 tablespoons chopped cilantro

1 clove garlic, minced

18 jalapeño peppers, cut lengthwise in half, seeds and membranes removed

MAKE IT

1. HEAT oven to 375°F. Mix all ingredients except peppers until well blended.

2. SPOON into peppers. Place, filled-sides up, on baking sheet.

3. BAKE 10 minutes or until cheese is melted.   *Makes 18 servings*

How to Handle Fresh Jalapeño Peppers: When handling fresh peppers, be sure to wear disposable rubber or clear plastic gloves to avoid irritating your skin. Never touch your eyes, nose or mouth when handling the peppers. If you've forgotten to wear the gloves and feel a burning sensation in your hands, apply a baking soda and water paste to the affected area. After rinsing the paste off, you should feel some relief.

Variation: Prepare using KRAFT® Shredded Monterey Jack Cheese.

Special Extra: Add ¼ teaspoon ground red pepper (cayenne) to the cream cheese mixture before spooning into peppers.

Prep Time: 20 minutes
Total Time: 30 minutes

Cheesy Spinach and Bacon Dip

WHAT YOU NEED

- 1 package (10 ounces) frozen chopped spinach, thawed, drained
- 1 pound (16 ounces) VELVEETA® Pasteurized Prepared Cheese Product, cut into ½-inch cubes
- 4 ounces (½ of 8-ounce package) PHILADELPHIA® Cream Cheese, cut up
- 1 can (10 ounces) RO*TEL® Diced Tomatoes & Green Chilies, undrained
- 8 slices OSCAR MAYER® Bacon, crisply cooked, drained and crumbled

MAKE IT

1. COMBINE ingredients in microwavable bowl.

2. MICROWAVE on HIGH 5 minutes or until VELVEETA® is completely melted and mixture is well blended, stirring after 3 minutes.

Makes 4 cups or 32 servings

How To Cut Up VELVEETA®: Cut VELVEETA® loaf into ½-inch-thick slices. Then cut each slice crosswise in both directions to make cubes.

Creative Leftovers: Cover and refrigerate any leftover dip. Then reheat and toss with your favorite hot cooked pasta.

Prep Time: 10 minutes
Total Time: 10 minutes

BLT Biscuits

2 cups all-purpose flour
2 teaspoons sugar
2 teaspoons baking powder
1 teaspoon black pepper
½ teaspoon baking soda
½ teaspoon salt
⅓ cup cold butter, cut into small pieces
1 cup (4 ounces) shredded Cheddar cheese
¾ cup buttermilk
1 package (16 ounces) bacon slices, crisp-cooked and
   cut crosswise into 3 pieces
1 small head romaine lettuce, torn into small pieces
4 plum tomatoes, cut into ¼-inch slices
½ cup mayonnaise

1. Preheat oven to 425°F. Line baking sheets with parchment paper.

2. Combine flour, sugar, baking powder, pepper, baking soda and salt in large bowl. Cut in butter with pastry blender or two knives until mixture resembles coarse crumbs. Stir in cheese and buttermilk just until mixture forms dough.

3. Turn dough out onto lightly floured surface; knead gently several times. Pat into 8×6-inch rectangle (about ¾ inch thick). Cut dough into 24 squares with sharp knife; place on prepared baking sheets. Bake 10 to 12 minutes or until golden brown. Cool slightly on wire rack.

4. Split biscuits; spread each half lightly with mayonnaise. Layer each biscuit with bacon, lettuce and tomato.   *Makes 24 mini sandwiches*

Turkey Club Biscuits: **Prepare BLT Biscuits as directed above, adding deli sliced turkey and avocado slices.**

Bacon-Wrapped Apricots

14 slices bacon, cut in half crosswise
¼ cup packed brown sugar
½ teaspoon black pepper
28 Mediterranean dried apricots (one 7-ounce package)
14 water chestnuts, drained and cut in half crosswise

1. Preheat oven to 425°F. Line shallow baking pan or baking sheet with parchment paper.

2. Sprinkle bacon with brown sugar and pepper, pressing to adhere. Fold apricot around water chestnut half. Wrap with half slice bacon; secure with toothpick.

3. Arrange apricots in prepared pan, spacing at least 1 inch apart. Bake about 20 minutes or until bacon is cooked through, turning once.

Makes 14 servings

Spicy Deviled Eggs

6 eggs
3 tablespoons whipping cream
1 green onion, finely chopped
1 tablespoon white wine vinegar
2 teaspoons Dijon mustard
½ teaspoon curry powder
½ teaspoon hot pepper sauce
3 tablespoons bacon, crisp-cooked and chopped
1 tablespoon chopped fresh chives (optional)

1. Place eggs in small saucepan; cover with cold water. Bring to a boil over high heat. Cover and remove from heat; let stand 15 minutes. Drain and rinse under cold water. Peel eggs; cool completely.

2. Slice eggs in half lengthwise. Remove yolks to small bowl; set whites aside. Mash yolks with fork. Stir in cream, green onion, vinegar, mustard, curry powder and pepper sauce until blended.

3. Spoon or pipe egg yolk mixture into centers of egg whites. Arrange eggs on serving plate. Sprinkle bacon over eggs. Garnish with chives.

Makes 12 deviled eggs

Crispy Bacon Sticks

½ cup (1½ ounces) grated Wisconsin Parmesan cheese,
  divided
5 slices bacon, halved lengthwise
10 breadsticks

MICROWAVE DIRECTIONS

Spread ¼ cup cheese on plate. Press one side of bacon into cheese; wrap diagonally around breadstick with cheese-coated side toward stick. Place on paper plate or microwave-safe baking sheet lined with paper towels. Repeat with remaining bacon halves, cheese and breadsticks. Microwave on HIGH 4 to 6 minutes or until bacon is cooked, checking for doneness after 4 minutes. Roll again in remaining ¼ cup Parmesan cheese. Serve warm. *Makes 10 sticks*

Favorite recipe from **Wisconsin Milk Marketing Board**

Hearty Calico Bean Dip

¾ pound ground beef
1 can (about 16 ounces) baked beans
1 can (about 15 ounces) Great Northern beans, rinsed and
  drained
1 can (about 15 ounces) kidney beans, rinsed and drained
½ pound bacon, crisp-cooked and crumbled
1 small onion, chopped
½ cup packed brown sugar
½ cup ketchup
1 tablespoon cider vinegar
1 teaspoon yellow mustard
  Tortilla chips

SLOW COOKER DIRECTIONS

1. Brown beef 6 to 8 minutes in large skillet over medium-high heat, stirring to break up meat. Drain fat. Transfer beef to slow cooker.

2. Add beans, bacon, onion, brown sugar, ketchup, vinegar and mustard to slow cooker; mix well.

3. Cover; cook on LOW 4 hours or on HIGH 2 hours. Serve with tortilla chips. *Makes 12 servings*

Roasted Red Potato Bites

  1½ pounds red potatoes (about 15 small)
   1 cup shredded Cheddar cheese (about 4 ounces)
   ½ cup HELLMANN'S® or BEST FOODS® Real Mayonnaise
   ½ cup sliced green onions
  10 slices bacon, crisp-cooked and crumbled
   2 tablespoons chopped fresh basil leaves (optional)

1. Preheat oven to 400°F. On large baking sheet, arrange potatoes and bake 35 minutes or until tender. Let stand until cool enough to handle.

2. Cut each potato in half, then cut thin slice from bottom of each potato half. With small melon baller or spoon, scoop pulp from potatoes leaving ¼-inch shell. Place pulp in medium bowl; set shells aside.

3. Lightly mash pulp. Stir in remaining ingredients. Spoon or pipe potato filling into potato shells.

4. Arrange filled shells on baking sheet and broil 3 minutes or until golden and heated through. *Makes 30 bites*

Prep Time: 10 minutes
Cook Time: 40 minutes

Oysters Romano

  12 oysters, shucked and on the half shell
   2 slices bacon, cut into 12 pieces
   ½ cup Italian seasoned dry bread crumbs
   2 tablespoons butter, melted
   ½ teaspoon garlic salt
   6 tablespoons grated Romano or Parmesan cheese
     Fresh chives (optional)

1. Preheat oven to 375°F. Place shells with oysters on baking sheet. Top each oyster with 1 piece bacon. Bake 10 minutes or until bacon is crisp.

2. Combine bread crumbs, butter and garlic salt in small bowl. Spoon mixture over oysters; sprinkle with cheese. Bake 5 minutes or until cheese is melted. Garnish with chives. *Makes 12 oysters*

Brandy-Soaked Scallops

1 pound bacon, cut in half crosswise
2 pounds small sea scallops
½ cup brandy
⅓ cup olive oil
2 tablespoons chopped fresh parsley
1 clove garlic, minced
1 teaspoon black pepper
½ teaspoon salt
½ teaspoon onion powder

1. Wrap one piece bacon around each scallop; secure with toothpick, if necessary. Place wrapped scallops in 13×9-inch baking dish.

2. Combine brandy, oil, parsley, garlic, pepper, salt and onion powder in small bowl; mix well. Pour mixture over scallops; cover and marinate in refrigerator at least 4 hours.

3. Remove scallops from marinade; discard marinade. Arrange scallops on rack of broiler pan. Broil 4 inches from heat 7 to 10 minutes or until bacon is browned. Turn; broil 5 minutes more or until scallops are opaque. Remove toothpicks. *Makes 8 servings*

Porky Pinwheels

1 sheet frozen puff pastry, thawed
1 egg white, beaten
8 slices bacon, crisp-cooked and crumbled
2 tablespoons packed brown sugar
¼ teaspoon ground red pepper

1. Place pastry on parchment paper. Brush with egg white.

2. Combine bacon, brown sugar and red pepper in small bowl. Sprinkle evenly over top; press lightly to adhere. Roll pastry jelly-roll style from long end. Wrap in parchment paper. Refrigerate 30 minutes.

3. Preheat oven to 400°F. Line baking sheet with parchment paper. Slice pastry into ½-inch-thick slices. Place 1 inch apart on prepared baking sheet.

4. Bake 10 minutes or until light golden brown. Remove to wire racks; cool completely. *Makes 24 pinwheels*

Alouette® Garlic and Herb Croustades

1 tablespoon olive oil
½ cup bacon, diced
1 cup baby bella or other mushrooms, chopped
⅔ cup chopped roasted red bell pepper
½ cup minced onion
1 teaspoon chopped garlic
1 (6.5-ounce) *or* 2 (4-ounce) packages ALOUETTE® Garlic & Herbs Spreadable Cheese
2 tablespoons fresh parsley *or* 1 tablespoon dried parsley flakes
2 (2-ounce) packages mini phyllo shells

In a nonstick pan over medium heat, heat oil and sauté the bacon for 3 to 5 minutes. Add mushrooms, pepper, onion and garlic. Continue sautéing for 3 to 5 minutes. Drain oil from the pan; reduce heat to low and add Alouette®. Blend and simmer for 1 minute. Remove from heat; stir in parsley. Spoon 1 heaping teaspoon into each phyllo shell; serve warm.

Makes 30 appetizers

 **BACON BITS**

For a creative touch, use any variety of seasonally fresh vegetables such as chopped fennel or squash.

SIZZLIN' SOUPS & SANDWICHES

Western Barbecue Burgers with Beer Barbecue Sauce

1½ pounds ground beef
1 cup smokehouse-style barbecue sauce
¼ cup brown ale
½ teaspoon salt
¼ teaspoon black pepper
1 red onion, cut into ½-inch-thick slices
4 hamburger buns
8 slices thick-sliced bacon, crisp-cooked
Lettuce leaves
Sliced tomatoes

1. Prepare grill for direct cooking. Shape beef into 4 patties about ¾ inch thick.

2. Combine barbecue sauce, ale, salt and pepper in small saucepan. Bring to a boil; boil 1 minute. Remove from heat; set aside.

3. Grill patties over medium-high heat, covered, 8 to 10 minutes (or uncovered, 13 to 15 minutes) until cooked through (160°F) or to desired doneness, turning occasionally. Grill onion 4 minutes or until softened and slightly charred, turning occasionally.

4. Place patties on bottom halves of buns; top with onion, bacon and barbecue sauce mixture. Place lettuce and tomatoes on top halves of buns.

Makes 4 servings

Bacon Potato Chowder

4 slices bacon, cooked and crumbled
1 large onion, chopped (about 1 cup)
4 cans (10¾ ounces each) **CAMPBELL'S®** Condensed Cream
of Potato Soup
4 soup cans milk
¼ teaspoon ground black pepper
2 large russet potatoes, cut into ½-inch pieces
(about 3 cups)
½ cup chopped fresh chives
2 cups shredded Cheddar cheese (about 8 ounces)

SLOW COOKER DIRECTIONS

1. Stir the bacon, onion, soup, milk, black pepper, potatoes and ¼ **cup** chives in a 6-quart slow cooker.

2. Cover and cook on HIGH for 3 to 4 hours or until the potatoes are tender.

3. Add the cheese and stir until the cheese is melted. Serve with the remaining chives.

Makes 8 servings

Cook Time: 3 to 4 hours

Toasted Cobb Salad Sandwiches

½ medium avocado
1 green onion, chopped
½ teaspoon lemon juice
   Salt and black pepper
2 kaiser rolls, split
4 ounces thinly sliced deli chicken or turkey
4 slices bacon, crisp-cooked
1 hard-cooked egg, sliced
2 slices (1 ounce each) Cheddar cheese
2 ounces blue cheese
   Olive oil

1. Mash avocado in small bowl; stir in green onion and lemon juice. Season with salt and pepper. Spread avocado mixture on cut sides of roll tops.

2. Layer bottoms of rolls with chicken, bacon, egg, Cheddar cheese and blue cheese. Close sandwiches with roll tops. Brush outsides of sandwiches lightly with olive oil.

3. Heat large nonstick skillet over medium heat. Add sandwiches; cook 4 to 5 minutes per side or until cheese melts and sandwiches are golden brown. *Makes 2 sandwiches*

Toasted Cobb Salad Sandwich

Simmered Split Pea Soup

3 cans (about 14 ounces each) chicken broth
1 package (16 ounces) dried split peas
8 slices bacon, crisp-cooked and chopped, divided
1 onion, diced
2 carrots, diced
1 teaspoon black pepper
½ teaspoon dried thyme
1 bay leaf

SLOW COOKER DIRECTIONS

1. Combine broth, peas, half of bacon, onion, carrots, pepper, thyme and bay leaf in slow cooker. Cover; cook on LOW 6 to 8 hours.

2. Remove and discard bay leaf; adjust seasonings, if desired. Garnish with remaining bacon.

Makes 6 servings

Prep Time: 15 minutes
Cook Time: 6 to 8 hours

Winter's Best Bean Soup

6 ounces bacon, crisp-cooked and diced
10 cups chicken broth
3 cans (about 15 ounces each) Great Northern beans, drained
1 can (about 14 ounces) diced tomatoes
1 large onion, chopped
1 package (about 10 ounces) frozen diced carrots
2 teaspoons minced garlic
1 fresh rosemary sprig *or* 1 teaspoon dried rosemary
1 teaspoon black pepper

SLOW COOKER DIRECTIONS

1. Layer all ingredients in slow cooker.

2. Cover; cook on LOW 8 hours. Remove rosemary sprig before serving.

Makes 8 to 10 servings

Prep Time: 15 minutes
Cook Time: 8 hours

Bacon & Tomato Melts

4 slices bacon, crisp-cooked
4 slices (1 ounce each) Cheddar cheese
1 medium tomato, sliced
4 slices whole wheat bread
2 tablespoons butter, melted

1. Layer 2 slices bacon, 2 slices cheese and tomato on each of 2 bread slices; top with remaining bread slices. Brush sandwiches with butter.

2. Heat large skillet over medium heat. Add sandwiches; press lightly with spatula. Cook 4 to 5 minutes per side or until cheese melts and sandwiches are golden brown. *Makes 2 sandwiches*

Chicken, Bacon and Vegetable Sandwiches

½ cup mayonnaise
¼ teaspoon garlic powder
½ teaspoon black pepper, divided
4 boneless skinless chicken breasts (about 1¼ pounds)
1 green bell pepper, cut into quarters
1 medium zucchini, cut lengthwise into 4 slices
3 tablespoons olive oil
2 cloves garlic, minced
1½ teaspoons dried basil
½ teaspoon salt
4 ciabatta or focaccia rolls, halved
2 Italian plum tomatoes, sliced
4 slices Provolone cheese
8 slices bacon, crisp-cooked

1. Preheat broiler. Combine mayonnaise, garlic powder and ¼ teaspoon black pepper in small bowl; set aside. Combine chicken, bell pepper, zucchini, oil, garlic, basil, salt and remaining ¼ teaspoon black pepper in large resealable food storage bag. Seal bag; knead to combine.

2. Broil chicken, bell pepper and zucchini 4 inches from heat 6 to 8 minutes on each side or until chicken is no longer pink in center. Layer bottom halves of rolls with mayonnaise mixture, zucchini, tomatoes, bell pepper, chicken, cheese, bacon and top halves of rolls.

Makes 4 sandwiches

Bacon & Tomato Melt

New England Fish Chowder

¼ pound bacon, diced
1 cup chopped onion
½ cup chopped celery
2 cups diced russet potatoes
2 tablespoons all-purpose flour
2 cups water
1 teaspoon salt
1 bay leaf
1 teaspoon dried dill
½ teaspoon dried thyme
½ teaspoon black pepper
1 pound cod, haddock or halibut fillets, skinned, boned and cut into 1-inch pieces
2 cups milk or half-and-half

1. Cook bacon in 5-quart Dutch oven over medium-high heat, stirring occasionally. Drain on paper towels.

2. Add onion and celery to drippings; cook and stir until onion is soft. Add potatoes; cook and stir 1 minute. Add flour; cook and stir 1 minute. Add water, salt, bay leaf, dill, thyme and pepper; bring to a boil over high heat. Reduce heat to low. Cover and simmer 25 minutes or until potatoes are fork-tender.

3. Add fish; simmer, covered, 5 minutes or until fish begins to flake when tested with fork. Discard bay leaf. Add bacon and milk; cook and stir until heated through. *Do not boil.*   *Makes 4 to 6 servings*

Mile-High Chicken Sandwich

1 tablespoon **HELLMANN'S®** or **BEST FOODS®** Real Mayonnaise
1 **ciabatta roll, split**
1 **cooked chicken breast (about 3 ounces)**
1 **slice bacon, crisp-cooked**
2 **slices tomato**
1 **ounce sliced Cheddar cheese**
   Green leaf lettuce

1. Spread HELLMANN'S® or BEST FOODS® Real Mayonnaise evenly on roll, then top with chicken, bacon, tomato, cheese and lettuce.

Makes 1 serving

Prep Time: 10 minutes

Bacon and Cheese Rarebit

1½ **tablespoons butter**
 ½ **cup beer (not dark)**
 2 **teaspoons** *each* **Worcestershire sauce and Dijon mustard**
 ⅛ **teaspoon ground red pepper**
 2 **cups (8 ounces) shredded American cheese**
1½ **cups (6 ounces) shredded sharp Cheddar cheese**
 1 **small loaf (8 ounces) egg bread or challah, cut into 6 (1-inch-thick) slices**
12 **large slices tomato**
12 **slices bacon, crisp-cooked**

1. Preheat broiler.

2. Melt butter in double boiler set over simmering water. Stir in beer, Worcestershire sauce, mustard and red pepper; heat through. Gradually add cheeses, stirring constantly, about 1 minute or until cheeses are melted. Remove from heat; cover and keep warm.

3. Broil bread slices until golden brown. Arrange on foil-lined baking sheet. Top each serving with tomato slices and bacon slices. Spoon cheese sauce evenly over top. Broil 4 to 5 inches from heat 2 to 3 minutes or until cheese sauce begins to brown. *Makes 6 servings*

Mile-High Chicken Sandwich

Baked Potato Soup

3 cans (10¾ ounces each) condensed cream of mushroom soup
4 cups milk
3 cups diced peeled baked potatoes
½ cup cooked crumbled bacon
1 tablespoon fresh thyme leaves *or* 1 teaspoon dried thyme leaves
   Sour cream and shredded Cheddar cheese
1½ cups *French's*® French Fried Onions

1. Combine soup and milk in large saucepan until blended. Stir in potatoes, bacon and thyme. Cook over medium heat about 10 to 15 minutes or until heated through, stirring frequently. Season to taste with salt and pepper.

2. Ladle soup into serving bowls. Top each serving with sour cream, cheese and 3 tablespoons French Fried Onions.   *Makes 8 servings*

Prep Time: 10 minutes
Cook Time: 15 minutes

Clam Chowder

5 cans (10¾ ounces each) condensed fat cream of potato soup, undiluted
2 cans (12 ounces each) evaporated milk
2 cans (10 ounces each) whole baby clams, rinsed and drained
1 can (about 14 ounces) cream-style corn
2 cans (4 ounces each) tiny shrimp, rinsed and drained
¾ cup bacon, crisp-cooked and crumbled
   Lemon pepper
   Oyster crackers

SLOW COOKER DIRECTIONS
1. Combine soup, evaporated milk, clams, corn, shrimp, bacon and lemon pepper in 4-quart slow cooker. Cover; cook on LOW 3 to 4 hours, stirring occasionally.
2. Serve with oyster crackers.   *Makes 10 servings*

Bacon and Blue Cheese Stuffed Burgers

4 slices applewood-smoked bacon or regular bacon
1 small red onion, finely chopped
2 tablespoons crumbled blue cheese
1 tablespoon butter, softened
1½ pounds ground beef
   Salt and black pepper
4 onion or plain hamburger rolls
   Lettuce leaves

1. Cook bacon in large skillet over medium-high heat until chewy but not crisp. Drain on paper towels. Chop into small pieces. Add onion to drippings in skillet; cook until soft. Cool.

2. Combine bacon, onion, blue cheese and butter in small bowl; mix well. Prepare grill for direct cooking.

3. Shape beef into 8 thin patties about 4 inches wide. Season patties with salt and pepper. Place 2 tablespoons bacon mixture in center of 1 patty; cover with another patty. Pinch edges together to seal. Shape burger until round and slightly flattened. Repeat with remaining patties and cheese mixture.

4. Grill patties over medium-high heat, covered, 8 to 10 minutes (or uncovered, 13 to 15 minutes) until cooked through (160°F) or to desired doneness, turning occasionally. Transfer burgers to platter; let stand 2 minutes before serving. Serve burgers on rolls with lettuce.

Makes 4 servings

 **BACON BITS**

If you want juicy, flavorful burgers, do not flatten patties. Pressing down on the patties with a spatula not only squeezes out tasty juices, but in this recipe it might also cause the stuffing to pop out.

Bacon and Blue Cheese Stuffed Burger

Tuscan White Bean Soup

10 cups chicken broth
1 package (16 ounces) dried Great Northern beans, rinsed and sorted
1 can (about 14 ounces) diced tomatoes
1 large onion, chopped
3 carrots, chopped
6 ounces bacon, crisp-cooked and diced
4 cloves garlic, minced
1 fresh rosemary sprig *or* 1 teaspoon dried rosemary
1 teaspoon black pepper

SLOW COOKER DIRECTIONS

1. Combine broth, beans, tomatoes, onion, carrots, bacon, garlic, rosemary and pepper to 5-quart slow cooker.

2. Cover; cook on LOW 8 hours. Remove and discard rosemary before serving.   *Makes 8 to 10 servings*

Serving Suggestion: Place slices of toasted Italian bread over individual servings. Drizzle with olive oil.

Peanut Butter BLT Wraps

½ cup **SKIPPY® Creamy, SUPER CHUNK® or Roasted Honey
  Nut Peanut Butter**
4 **fajita-size flour tortillas**
8 **slices bacon, crisp-cooked**
4 **lettuce leaves**
1 **large tomato, sliced**

1. Evenly spread SKIPPY® Creamy Peanut Butter over tortillas, then evenly top with remaining ingredients; roll up. To serve, cut each wrap in half. *Makes 4 servings*

Prep Time: 5 minutes

Deluxe Bacon & Gouda Burgers

1½ **pounds ground beef**
⅓ **cup mayonnaise**
1 **teaspoon minced garlic**
¼ **teaspoon Dijon mustard**
2 **thick red onion slices**
  Salt and black pepper
4 to 8 **slices Gouda cheese**
  Butter lettuce leaves
4 **onion rolls, split and toasted**
  Tomato slices
4 to 8 **slices bacon, crisp-cooked**

1. Prepare grill for direct cooking. Shape beef into 4 patties about ¾-inch thick. Cover and refrigerate. Combine mayonnaise, garlic and mustard in small bowl; mix well.

2. Grill patties and onions over medium-high heat, covered, 8 to 10 minutes (or uncovered, 13 to 15 minutes) until cooked through (160°F) or to desired doneness, turning occasionally. Remove onion when slightly browned. Season burgers with salt and pepper. Top with cheese during last 2 minutes of grilling.

3. Arrange lettuce on bottom half of each roll; top with mayonnaise mixture, burger, onion, tomato and bacon. Cover with top halves of rolls.

Makes 4 servings

Leek and Potato Soup

5 cups shredded frozen hash brown potatoes

3 leeks, white and light green parts only, cut into ¾-inch
pieces

1 can (10¾ ounces) condensed cream of potato soup,
undiluted

1 can (about 14 ounces) chicken broth

6 slices bacon, crisp-cooked and chopped, divided

2 ribs celery, sliced

1 can (5 ounces) evaporated milk

½ cup sour cream

SLOW COOKER DIRECTIONS

1. Combine potatoes, leeks, soup, broth, all but 2 tablespoons bacon,
celery and evaporated milk in slow cooker. Cover; cook on LOW 6 to
7 hours.

2. Stir in sour cream. Sprinkle with reserved bacon.

Makes 4 to 6 servings

Grilled Chicken Sandwiches with Basil Spread with Real Mayonnaise

⅓ cup **HELLMANN'S®** or **BEST FOODS®** Real Mayonnaise
¼ cup finely chopped fresh basil leaves
¼ cup grated Parmesan cheese
8 slices whole-grain bread
1 pound boneless, skinless chicken breast halves, grilled and sliced
8 slices tomato
4 slices bacon, crisp-cooked and halved crosswise

1. Combine HELLMANN'S® or BEST FOODS® Real Mayonnaise, basil and cheese in small bowl. Evenly spread mixture on bread slices. Equally top 4 bread slices with chicken, tomato and bacon, then top with remaining bread. *Makes 4 servings*

Prep Time: 25 minutes

Bacon Burgers

8 slices bacon, crisp-cooked and divided
4 pounds ground beef
1½ teaspoons chopped fresh thyme *or* ½ teaspoon dried thyme
½ teaspoon salt
Dash black pepper
4 slices Swiss cheese

1. Prepare grill for direct cooking. Crumble 4 slices bacon.

2. Combine beef, crumbled bacon, thyme, salt and pepper in medium bowl; mix lightly. Shape into 4 patties.

3. Grill patties over medium-high heat, covered, 8 to 10 minutes (or uncovered, 13 to 15 minutes) until cooked through (160°F) or to desired doneness, turning occasionally. Top with cheese during last 2 minutes of grilling. Serve with remaining bacon slices. *Makes 4 servings*

Grilled Chicken Sandwich with Basil Spread with Real Mayonnaise

Oyster Chowder

4 slices thick-cut bacon, diced
1¼ cups chopped onion
1 can (about 14 ounces) chicken or vegetable broth
1¼ cups diced peeled potato
1 pint fresh shucked oysters, drained, liquor reserved
1 cup whipping cream or half-and-half
Salt and black pepper
Sliced green onions (optional)

1. Cook bacon in large saucepan over medium heat until crisp, stirring frequently. Drain on paper towels.

2. Drain all but 2 tablespoons drippings. Add onion to skillet; cook and stir 5 minutes or until tender.

3. Add broth, potato and oyster liquor; increase heat to high. Cover and simmer 5 minutes or until potato is tender but firm. Stir in oysters and cream; cook 5 minutes or until edges of oysters begin to curl.

4. Season with salt and pepper. Ladle into bowls; top with bacon and green onions. *Makes 4 (⅔-cup) servings*

BACON-LICIOUS MAIN DISHES

Pork Meatballs & Sauerkraut

1¼ pounds ground pork
¾ cup dry bread crumbs
1 egg, lightly beaten
2 tablespoons milk
2 teaspoons caraway seeds, divided
1 teaspoon salt
½ teaspoon Worcestershire sauce
¼ teaspoon black pepper
1 jar (32 ounces) sauerkraut, drained, squeezed dry and snipped
6 slices bacon, crisp-cooked and crumbled
½ cup chopped onion
  Chopped fresh parsley (optional)

SLOW COOKER DIRECTIONS

1. Combine pork, bread crumbs, egg, milk, 1 teaspoon caraway seeds, salt, Worcestershire sauce and pepper in large bowl. Shape mixture into 2-inch balls. Brown meatballs in large nonstick skillet over medium-high heat.

2. Combine sauerkraut, bacon, onion and remaining 1 teaspoon caraway seeds in slow cooker. Place meatballs on top of sauerkraut mixture.

3. Cover; cook on LOW 6 to 8 hours. Sprinkle with parsley.

Makes 4 to 6 servings

Prep Time: 30 minutes
Cook Time: 6 to 8 hours

Spaghetti Bolognese

6 slices bacon, cut into ½-inch pieces
1 large onion, diced (about 1 cup)
3 cloves garlic, minced
2 pounds ground beef
4 cups PREGO® Traditional Italian Sauce
1 cup milk
1 pound spaghetti, cooked and drained*
   Grated Parmesan cheese

Reserve some of the cooking water from the spaghetti. You can use it to adjust the consistency of the finished sauce, if you like.

1. Cook the bacon in a 12-inch skillet over medium-high heat until it's crisp. Remove the bacon from the skillet. Pour off all but **1 tablespoon** of the drippings.

2. Add the onion and cook in the hot drippings until tender. Add the garlic and beef and cook until the beef is well browned, stirring often. Pour off any fat.

3. Stir the bacon, beef mixture, Italian sauce and milk in a 6-quart slow cooker.

4. Cover and cook on HIGH for 4 to 5 hours.** Toss the spaghetti with the sauce. Sprinkle with the cheese, as desired.   *Makes 8 servings*

**Or on LOW for 7 to 8 hours.*

Cook Time: 4 hours
Prep Time: 15 minutes
Total Time: 4 hours 15 minutes

Farm-Raised Catfish with Bacon and Horseradish

6 (4- to 5-ounce) farm-raised catfish fillets
2 tablespoons butter
¼ cup chopped onion
1 (8-ounce) package cream cheese, softened
¼ cup dry white wine
2 tablespoons prepared horseradish
1 tablespoon Dijon mustard
½ teaspoon salt
⅛ teaspoon black pepper
4 strips bacon, crisp-cooked and crumbled
    Lettuce leaves (optional)

1. Preheat oven to 350°F. Grease large baking dish. Arrange fillets in single layer in prepared dish.

2. Melt butter in small skillet over medium-high heat. Add onion; cook and stir until softened. Combine cream cheese, wine, horseradish, mustard, salt and pepper in small bowl; stir in onion. Pour over fish and top with crumbled bacon.

3. Bake 30 minutes or until fish begins to flake when tested with fork. Serve immediately on lettuce leaves.   *Makes 6 servings*

Brisket with Bacon, Blue Cheese and Onions

2 large sweet onions,* sliced into ½-inch rounds
6 slices bacon
1 flat-cut boneless beef brisket (about 3½ pounds)
    Salt and black pepper
2 cans (10½ ounces each) condensed beef consommé, undiluted
1 teaspoon cracked black peppercorns
3 ounces crumbled blue cheese

*Maui, Vidalia or Walla Walla onions are preferred.

SLOW COOKER DIRECTIONS

1. Coat 5- to 6-quart slow cooker with nonstick cooking spray. Line bottom with onion slices.

2. Heat large skillet over medium-high heat. Add bacon and cook until chewy but not crisp. Drain on paper towels. Chop bacon.

3. Season brisket with salt and pepper. Sear brisket in bacon drippings on all sides. Transfer to slow cooker.

4. Pour consommé in slow cooker. Sprinkle with peppercorns and half of bacon. Cover; cook on HIGH 5 to 7 hours.

5. Transfer brisket to cutting board; let stand 10 minutes. Slice against the grain into ¾-inch slices.

6. To serve, arrange brisket slices on plates; top with onions, blue cheese and remaining bacon. Season cooking liquid with salt and pepper; serve with brisket.

Makes 6 to 8 servings

Prep Time: 15 minutes
Cook Time: 5 to 7 hours

Tortellini Carbonara

1 package (15 ounces) cheese tortellini
1 box (10 ounces) frozen broccoli florets, thawed
1 jar (1 pound) RAGÚ® Cheesy! Roasted Garlic Parmesan
   Sauce
½ cup diced drained roasted red peppers
4 ounces bacon, crisp-cooked and crumbled

1. In 3-quart saucepan, cook tortellini according to package directions, adding broccoli during last 2 minutes of cooking; drain. Return pasta mixture to saucepan. Stir in Ragú Cheesy! Roasted Garlic Parmesan Sauce and peppers. Spoon onto platter and top with bacon. Garnish, if desired, with Parmesan cheese. *Makes 4 servings*

Macaroni & Cheese with Bacon

3 cups (8 ounces) uncooked rotini pasta
2 tablespoons butter
2 tablespoons all-purpose flour
¼ teaspoon salt
¼ teaspoon dry mustard
⅛ teaspoon black pepper
1½ cups milk
2 cups (8 ounces) shredded sharp Cheddar cheese
8 ounces bacon, crisp-cooked and crumbled
2 medium tomatoes, sliced

1. Preheat oven to 350°F. Lightly grease shallow 1½-quart casserole.

2. Cook pasta according to package directions; drain and return to saucepan.

3. Melt butter in medium saucepan over medium-low heat. Whisk in flour, salt, mustard and pepper; cook and stir 1 minute. Whisk in milk. Bring to a boil over medium heat, stirring frequently. Reduce heat and simmer 2 minutes. Remove from heat. Add cheese; stir until melted.

4. Add cheese mixture and bacon to pasta; stir until well blended. Transfer to prepared casserole. Bake, uncovered, 20 minutes. Arrange tomato slices on casserole. Bake 5 to 8 minutes or until casserole is bubbly and cooked through. *Makes 4 servings*

Bacon, Onion & Stout Braised Short Ribs

4 pounds bone-in beef short ribs, well trimmed

1 teaspoon salt, plus additional for seasoning

½ teaspoon ground black pepper, plus additional for seasoning

1 tablespoon vegetable oil

6 ounces thick-cut bacon, chopped

1 large onion, halved and cut into slices

1 tablespoon tomato paste

2 tablespoons all-purpose flour

2 tablespoons spicy brown mustard

1 bottle (12 ounces) Irish stout

1 cup beef broth

1 bay leaf

2 tablespoons finely chopped parsley

Hot mashed potatoes

SLOW COOKER DIRECTIONS

1. Season ribs with salt and pepper. Heat oil in large skillet over medium-high heat until almost smoking. Cook ribs in batches, turning to brown all sides. Transfer each batch to slow cooker. Wipe skillet with paper towels.

2. Cook bacon in same skillet over medium heat about 4 minutes or until crisp, stirring occasionally. Drain on paper towels. Drain all but 1 tablespoon drippings from pan.

3. Add onion to drippings in skillet; cook and stir until softened and translucent. Add tomato paste, flour, mustard, 1 teaspoon salt and ½ teaspoon pepper; cook and stir 1 minute. Remove skillet from heat and pour in stout, stirring to scrape up browned bits. Pour over short ribs. Add bacon, broth and bay leaf.

4. Cover; cook on LOW 8 hours.

5. Skim fat from cooking liquid. Remove bay leaf; stir in parsley. Serve with mashed potatoes.   *Makes 4 to 6 servings*

Cook's Tip: This recipe only gets better if made ahead and refrigerated overnight. This makes skimming any fat from the surface easier, too.

Macaroni and Cheese Dijon

WHAT YOU NEED

1¼ cups milk

½ pound (8 ounces) VELVEETA® Pasteurized Prepared Cheese Product, cut into ½-inch cubes

2 tablespoons GREY POUPON® Dijon Mustard

6 slices OSCAR MAYER® Bacon, cooked, drained and crumbled

⅓ cup green onion slices

⅛ teaspoon ground red pepper (cayenne)

3½ cups tri-colored rotini pasta, cooked and drained

½ cup French fried onion rings

MAKE IT

1. PREHEAT oven to 350°F. Mix milk, VELVEETA® and mustard in medium saucepan; cook on low heat until VELVEETA® is completely melted and mixture is well blended, stirring occasionally. Add bacon, green onions and pepper; mix lightly. Remove from heat. Add to pasta in large bowl; toss to coat.

2. SPOON into greased 2-quart casserole dish; cover.

3. BAKE 15 to 20 minutes or until heated through. Uncover; stir. Top with onion rings. Bake, uncovered, an additional 5 minutes. Let stand 10 minutes before serving. *Makes 6 servings, 1 cup each*

Prep Time: 20 minutes
Total Time: 45 minutes

BACON BITS

For easy crumbled bacon, use kitchen scissors to snip raw bacon into ½-inch pieces. Let pieces fall right into skillet, then cook until crisp and drain on paper towels.

Chicken and Bacon Skewers

¼ cup lemon juice
¼ cup soy sauce
2 tablespoons brown sugar
1½ teaspoons lemon pepper
2 boneless skinless chicken breasts (about ½ pound), cut into 1-inch cubes
1 teaspoon coarsely ground black pepper
½ pound bacon, cut in half crosswise
Lemon wedges (optional)

1. Combine lemon juice, soy sauce, brown sugar and lemon pepper in large resealable food storage bag; mix well. Remove ¼ cup marinade; set aside. Add chicken to bag; seal. Marinate in refrigerator at least 30 minutes. Preheat broiler.

2. Sprinkle black pepper over bacon; gently press to adhere. Fold each slice in half. Remove chicken from bag; discard marinade. Alternately thread chicken and bacon onto skewers.

3. Broil skewers 10 to 15 minutes or until chicken is no longer pink in center and bacon is crisp, turning occasionally. Brush several times with reserved marinade. Garnish with lemon wedges.   *Makes 2 servings*

Note: If using wooden skewers, soak in water 20 to 30 minutes before using to prevent scorching.

Gypsy's BBQ Chicken

6 boneless skinless chicken breasts (about 1½ pounds)
1 bottle (26 ounces) barbecue sauce
6 slices bacon, crisp-cooked and halved
6 slices Swiss cheese

SLOW COOKER DIRECTIONS

1. Place chicken in slow cooker. Cover with barbecue sauce. Cover; cook on LOW 8 to 9 hours.

2. Place 2 slices cooked bacon over each piece of chicken in slow cooker. Top with cheese. Cover; cook on HIGH until cheese melts.

Makes 6 servings

Beer and Kraut Brats

½ pound thick-cut bacon, diced
1 pound bratwurst, cut into 2-inch pieces
1 can (12 fluid ounces) beer
1 can (10¾ ounces) CAMPBELL'S® Condensed French
    Onion Soup
¼ cup packed brown sugar
1 package (16 ounces) fresh sauerkraut, drained
    (about 3 cups)
    Hot mashed potatoes

1. Cook bacon in a 12-inch skillet over medium-high heat for 5 minutes or until the bacon is crisp. Remove the bacon with a slotted spoon and drain on paper towels. Pour off drippings.

2. Add the bratwurst and cook until it's well browned.

3. Add the beer, soup, brown sugar, sauerkraut and bacon. Heat to a boil. Reduce the heat to low.

4. Cook for 15 minutes or until the bratwurst reaches an internal temperature of 160°F., stirring the mixture a few times while it is cooking. Serve over potatoes.   *Makes 4 servings*

Prep Time: 10 minutes
Cook Time: 25 minutes

Sweet and Salty Salmon

4 skinless salmon fillets (6 ounces each)
1 tablespoon brown sugar, divided
4 slices bacon

1. Preheat oven to 350°F. Place wire rack on top of baking sheet. Place salmon on wire rack; rub half of brown sugar on tops of salmon.

2. Cut each slice of bacon crosswise into 2 pieces. Lay 2 pieces of bacon over brown sugar, overlapping slightly. Sprinkle with remaining brown sugar.

3. Bake 15 minutes or until bacon is crisp and salmon begins to flake when tested with fork.

Makes 4 servings

Bacon & Tomato Presto Pasta

WHAT YOU NEED

8 slices OSCAR MAYER® Bacon, chopped
½ cup cherry tomatoes
1 tub (8 ounces) PHILADELPHIA® Chive & Onion Cream Cheese Spread
1 cup milk
½ cup KRAFT® 100% Grated Parmesan Cheese
6 cups hot cooked penne pasta

MAKE IT

1. COOK bacon in skillet 5 minutes or until bacon is crisp, stirring occasionally. Drain skillet, leaving bacon in skillet. Stir in cherry tomatoes.

2. ADD cream cheese spread, milk and Parmesan cheese; mix well. Cook until hot and bubbly, stirring frequently. Stir in pasta.

Makes 8 servings

Prep Time: 10 minutes
Cook Time: 10 minutes

Fettuccine alla Carbonara

12 ounces uncooked fettuccine
 4 ounces bacon, cut crosswise into ½-inch pieces
 3 cloves garlic, cut into halves
 ¼ cup dry white wine
 ⅓ cup whipping cream
 1 egg
 1 egg yolk
 ⅔ cup grated Parmesan cheese, divided
   Dash white pepper

1. Cook fettuccine according to package directions. Drain; cover and keep warm.

2. Cook and stir bacon and garlic in large skillet over medium-low heat 4 minutes or until lightly browned. Drain and discard garlic and all but 2 tablespoons drippings from skillet.

3. Add wine to skillet; cook over medium heat 3 minutes or until wine is almost evaporated. Add cream; cook and stir 2 minutes. Remove from heat.

4. Whisk egg and egg yolk in top of double boiler. Place top of double boiler over simmering water, adjusting heat to maintain simmer. Whisk ⅓ cup cheese and pepper into egg mixture; cook and stir until sauce is thickened.

5. Pour bacon mixture over fettuccine; toss to coat. Cook over medium-low heat until heated through. Add egg mixture; toss to coat. Serve with remaining ⅓ cup cheese.

Makes 4 servings

Baked Chicken with Bacon-Tomato Sauce

2 cups fire-roasted diced tomatoes*
4 pounds bone-in chicken pieces
¾ teaspoon salt, divided
¼ teaspoon black pepper
6 slices bacon, cut into 1-inch pieces
1 onion, cut into ½-inch pieces

*Fire-roasted tomatoes give this dish a deeper, more complex flavor. Look for them in your supermarket or specialty store next to the other canned tomato products.

1. Preheat oven to 450°F. Spread tomatoes on bottom of 13×9-inch baking dish.

2. Season chicken with ½ teaspoon salt and pepper. Coat large nonstick skillet with cooking spray; heat over medium-high heat. Add chicken; cook 8 minutes or until browned and crisp, turning once. Transfer to baking dish. Bake 30 to 40 minutes or until chicken is cooked through (165°F).

3. Meanwhile, cook bacon in same skillet over medium-high heat about 8 minutes or until crisp, stirring once. Drain on paper towels. Reserve drippings in skillet.

4. Cook onion in drippings 8 minutes or until golden, stirring occasionally. Drain fat. Stir in remaining ¼ teaspoon salt.

5. Top chicken and tomatoes with bacon and onions.

Makes 4 servings

CRACKLIN' GOOD SIDES & SALADS

Roast Herbed Sweet Potatoes with Bacon & Onions

3 thick slices applewood-smoked or peppered bacon, diced
2 pounds sweet potatoes, peeled and cut into 2-inch chunks
2 medium onions, cut into 8 wedges
1 teaspoon salt
1 teaspoon dried thyme
¼ teaspoon black pepper
   Fresh thyme sprig (optional)

1. Preheat oven to 375°F.

2. Cook bacon in large deep skillet until crisp. Drain on paper towels.

3. Add potatoes and onions to drippings in skillet; toss until coated. Stir in salt, dried thyme and pepper. Spread mixture in single layer in ungreased 15×10-inch jelly-roll pan or shallow roasting pan.

4. Bake 40 to 50 minutes or until golden brown and tender. Transfer vegetables to serving bowl; sprinkle with bacon. Garnish with thyme sprig.

Makes 10 to 12 servings

Spinach Salad with Italian Marinated Mushrooms & Gorgonzola

½ cup **WISH-BONE®** Italian or Light Italian Dressing, divided
1 package (10 ounces) cremini or white mushrooms, washed and stems trimmed
1 small red onion, sliced into ½-inch rounds
1 package (10 ounces) baby spinach or (4 ounces) baby arugula
1 package (4 ounces) Gorgonzola cheese crumbles*
4 slices bacon, crisp-cooked and crumbled
Freshly ground black pepper (optional)

Also terrific with blue cheese crumbles.

Pour ¼ cup WISH-BONE® Italian Dressing over mushrooms and onion in medium nonaluminum baking dish or resealable plastic bag. Cover or close bag and marinate in refrigerator, turning occasionally, at least 30 minutes.

Remove vegetables from marinade, reserving marinade. Grill or broil vegetables, brushing with reserved marinade, 15 minutes or until tender. Quarter mushrooms and chop onion; let stand, covered, in medium bowl, then toss with remaining ¼ cup Dressing.

Toss spinach, mushroom mixture with juices, cheese and bacon in large serving bowl or platter. Sprinkle with black pepper.   *Makes 6 servings*

Prep Time: 15 minutes
Marinate Time: 30 minutes
Cook Time: 15 minutes

Bacon-Cheese Grits

2 cups milk
½ cup quick-cooking grits
1½ cups (6 ounces) shredded sharp Cheddar cheese *or*
    6 slices American cheese, torn into bite-size pieces
2 tablespoons butter
1 teaspoon Worcestershire sauce
½ teaspoon salt
⅛ teaspoon ground red pepper (optional)
4 thick-cut slices bacon, crisp-cooked and chopped

1. Bring milk to a boil in large saucepan over medium-high heat. Slowly stir in grits. Return to a boil. Reduce heat. Cover; simmer 5 minutes, stirring frequently.

2. Remove grits from heat. Stir in cheese, butter, Worcestershire sauce, salt and red pepper, if desired. Cover; let stand 2 minutes or until cheese is melted. Top each serving with bacon.   *Makes 4 (¾-cup) servings*

Variation: For a thinner consistency, add ½ cup milk.

Red Cabbage and Apples

1 small head red cabbage, cored and thinly sliced
3 medium apples, peeled and grated
¾ cup sugar
½ cup red wine vinegar
1 teaspoon ground cloves
1 cup bacon, crisp-cooked and crumbled
    Fresh apple slices (optional)

SLOW COOKER DIRECTIONS
1. Combine cabbage, apples, sugar, vinegar and cloves in slow cooker. Cover; cook on HIGH 6 hours, stirring after 3 hours.

2. Sprinkle with bacon. Garnish with apple slices.
                                        Makes 4 to 6 servings

Garden Vegetable Pasta Salad with Bacon

12 ounces uncooked rotini pasta
 2 cups broccoli florets
 1 can (about 14 ounces) diced tomatoes
 2 medium carrots, diagonally sliced
 2 stalks celery, sliced
10 medium mushrooms, thinly sliced
 ½ medium red onion, thinly sliced
 ½ pound bacon, crisp-cooked and thinly sliced
 1 bottle (8 ounces) Italian or ranch salad dressing
 ½ cup (2 ounces) shredded Cheddar cheese
 1 tablespoon dried parsley
 2 teaspoons dried basil
 ¼ teaspoon black pepper

1. Cook pasta according to package directions. Drain and rinse well under cold water until cool.

2. Combine broccoli, tomatoes, carrots, celery, mushrooms and onion in large bowl. Add pasta and bacon; toss lightly.

3. Add salad dressing, cheese, parsley, basil and pepper; stir to combine.

Makes 6 servings

Prep and Cook Time: 25 minutes

Five-Bean Casserole

2 medium onions, chopped

8 ounces bacon, diced

2 cloves garlic, minced

½ cup packed brown sugar

½ cup cider vinegar

1 teaspoon salt

1 teaspoon dry mustard

¼ teaspoon black pepper

2 cans (about 15 ounces each) kidney beans, rinsed and drained

1 can (about 15 ounces) chickpeas, rinsed and drained

1 can (about 15 ounces) butter beans, rinsed and drained

1 can (about 15 ounces) Great Northern or cannellini beans, rinsed and drained

1 can (about 15 ounces) baked beans

SLOW COOKER DIRECTIONS

1. Cook and stir onions, bacon and garlic in large skillet over medium heat until onions are tender; drain. Stir in brown sugar, vinegar, salt, mustard and pepper. Simmer over low heat 15 minutes.

2. Combine kidney beans, chickpeas, butter beans, Great Northern beans and baked beans in slow cooker. Spoon onion mixture evenly over top. Cover; cook on LOW 6 to 8 hours or on HIGH 3 to 4 hours.

Makes 16 servings

 **BACON BITS**

Bacon is highly perishable and should be used soon after purchasing. It will keep in the refrigerator about 10 days or can be frozen up to 3 months.

Turkey Club Salad

8 cups coarsely chopped romaine lettuce leaves
2 large hard-cooked eggs, diced
1 cup cherry tomatoes, halved
4 slices bacon, crisp-cooked and crumbled
1 package (4 ounces) blue cheese crumbles
8 slices deli turkey breast, rolled-up
½ cup **WISH-BONE®** Ranch Dressing

Arrange lettuce on large platter. Top with rows of eggs, tomatoes, bacon, cheese and turkey. Just before serving, drizzle with WISH-BONE® Ranch Dressing.

Makes 4 servings

Prep Time: 15 minutes

Market Salad

3 eggs
4 cups mixed baby salad greens
2 cups green beans, cut into 1½-inch pieces, cooked and drained
4 thick slices bacon, crisp-cooked and crumbled
1 tablespoon minced fresh basil, chives or Italian parsley
3 tablespoons olive oil
1 tablespoon red wine vinegar
1 teaspoon Dijon mustard
    Salt and black pepper

1. Place eggs in small saucepan with enough water to cover; bring to a boil over medium-high heat. Immediately remove from heat. Cover; let stand 10 minutes. Drain; cool eggs to room temperature.

2. Combine salad greens, green beans, bacon and basil in large serving bowl. Peel and coarsely chop eggs; add to serving bowl. Combine oil, vinegar, mustard, salt and pepper in small bowl; drizzle over salad. Toss gently to coat.

Makes 4 servings

Easy Cheesy Potatoes

WHAT YOU NEED

1 pound russet potatoes (about 4 medium), cut into ½-inch chunks

½ pound (8 ounces) VELVEETA® Pasteurized Prepared Cheese Product, cut up

½ cup chopped onions

¼ cup KRAFT® Real Mayo Mayonnaise

4 slices OSCAR MAYER® Bacon, cooked, drained and crumbled (about ½ cup)

MAKE IT

1. HEAT oven to 375°F. Combine all ingredients except bacon in 8-inch square baking dish sprayed with cooking spray; cover with foil.

2. BAKE 45 minutes.

3. TOP with bacon; bake, uncovered, 5 to 10 minutes or until potatoes are tender. *Makes 10 servings*

Special Extra: Sprinkle with 1 tablespoon chopped fresh parsley just before serving.

Prep Time: 15 minutes
Total Time: 1 hour 10 minutes

Cobb Salad

1 package (10 ounces) torn mixed salad greens *or* 8 cups
   torn romaine lettuce
6 ounces deli chicken, turkey or smoked turkey breast, diced
1 large tomato, seeded and chopped
⅓ cup bacon, crisp-cooked and crumbled
1 large ripe avocado, peeled and diced
   Blue cheese
   Prepared blue cheese or Caesar salad dressing

1. Place lettuce in salad bowl. Arrange chicken, tomato, bacon and avocado in rows.

2. Sprinkle with blue cheese. Serve with dressing.   *Makes 4 servings*

Serving Suggestion: Serve with warm French or Italian rolls.

Prep Time: 15 minutes

Spinach Salad with Beets

6 cups packed baby spinach or torn spinach leaves
   (6 ounces)
1 cup well-drained canned pickled julienned beets
¼ cup thinly sliced red onion, separated into rings
¼ cup croutons
⅓ cup raspberry vinaigrette salad dressing
¼ cup bacon, crisp-cooked and crumbled
   Black pepper (optional)

1. Combine spinach, beets, onion and croutons in large bowl. Add dressing; toss to coat.

2. Sprinkle with bacon and pepper, if desired.   *Makes 4 (2-cup) servings*

Bacon-Jalapeño Corn Bread

4 slices bacon
¼ cup minced green onions
2 jalapeño peppers,* stemmed, seeded and minced
1 cup all-purpose flour
1 cup yellow cornmeal
2½ teaspoons baking powder
¾ teaspoon salt
½ teaspoon baking soda
1 egg
¾ cup plain yogurt
¾ cup milk
¼ cup (½ stick) butter, melted
½ cup (2 ounces) shredded Cheddar cheese

*Jalapeño peppers can sting and irritate the skin, so wear rubber gloves when handling peppers and do not touch your eyes.

1. Preheat oven to 400°F.

2. Cook bacon in large skillet over medium heat until crisp. Drain on paper towels. Pour 2 tablespoons drippings into 9-inch square baking pan or cast iron skillet.

3. Crumble bacon into small bowl; add green onions and jalapeños. Combine flour, cornmeal, baking powder, salt and baking soda in large bowl.

4. Beat egg slightly in medium bowl; add yogurt and whisk until smooth. Whisk in milk and butter. Pour egg mixture into dry ingredients; stir just until moistened. Stir in bacon mixture. Pour into prepared pan; sprinkle with cheese.

5. Bake 20 to 25 minutes or until toothpick inserted into center comes out clean. Cut into squares or wedges. *Makes 9 to 12 servings*

BLT Salad with Bow Ties & Cheddar

2 cups (4 ounces) bow tie or corkscrew-shaped pasta
1 package (9 ounces) DOLE® Classic Romaine Salad Blend or Baby Spinach Salad
1 cup cherry, pear or baby Roma tomatoes, halved
¾ cup (3 ounces) Cheddar cheese, diced
5 strips bacon, cooked, drained and crumbled _or_ ⅓ cup packaged bacon bits
⅓ cup ranch salad dressing

• Cook pasta according to package directions. Drain well and rinse in cool water. Drain again.

• Toss together salad blend, pasta, tomatoes, cheese and bacon in large bowl. Pour dressing over salad; toss to evenly coat.

Makes 3 to 4 servings

Prep Time: 20 minutes
Cook Time: 10 to 16 minutes

Country-Style Corn

4 slices bacon
1 tablespoon flour
1 can (about 15 ounces) corn, drained
1 can (about 15 ounces) cream-style corn
1 red bell pepper, diced
½ cup sliced green onions
Salt and black pepper

1. Cook bacon in large skillet over medium heat until crisp; drain on paper towels. Crumble bacon; set aside.

2. Whisk flour into drippings. Add corn, cream-style corn and bell pepper to skillet; bring to a boil. Reduce heat to low; cook 10 minutes or until thickened.

3. Stir green onions and bacon into corn mixture. Season with salt and black pepper.

Makes 6 to 8 servings

Bacon Roasted Brussels Sprouts

1 pound Brussels sprouts
3 slices bacon, cut into ½-inch pieces
2 teaspoons brown sugar
  Salt and black pepper

1. Preheat oven to 400°F. Trim ends from Brussels sprouts; cut in half lengthwise.

2. Combine Brussels sprouts, bacon and brown sugar in glass baking dish.

3. Roast 25 to 30 minutes or until golden brown, stirring once. Season with salt and pepper. *Makes 4 servings*

Grilled Shrimp Salad with Hot Bacon Vinaigrette

4 strips bacon, chopped
½ cup prepared Italian or vinaigrette salad dressing
⅓ cup *French's*® Honey Dijon Mustard or *French's*® Honey
    Mustard
2 tablespoons water
8 cups mixed salad greens
1 cup diced yellow bell peppers
1 cup halved cherry tomatoes
½ cup pine nuts
1 pound jumbo or extra large shrimp, shelled, with
    tails left on

1. Cook bacon until crisp in medium skillet. Whisk in salad dressing, mustard and water; keep warm over very low heat.

2. Place salad greens, bell peppers, tomatoes and pine nuts in large bowl; toss. Arrange on salad plates.

3. Cook shrimp in an electric grill pan or barbecue grill 3 minutes or until pink. Arrange on salads, dividing evenly. Serve with dressing.

Makes 4 servings

Prep Time: 10 minutes
Cook Time: 5 minutes

Loaded Grilled Potato Packet

REYNOLDS WRAP® Non-Stick Foil
4 medium potatoes, cut into ½-inch cubes
1 large onion, diced
2 tablespoons olive oil
4 slices bacon, cooked and crumbled
2 teaspoons seasoned salt
1 tablespoon chopped fresh chives
1 cup shredded Cheddar cheese
Sour cream (optional)

PREHEAT grill to medium-high or oven to 450°F.

CENTER potatoes and onion on sheet of Reynolds Wrap Non-Stick Foil with non-stick (dull) side toward food. Drizzle with olive oil. Sprinkle with crumbled bacon, seasoned salt, chives and cheese.

BRING up foil sides. Double fold top and ends to seal, making one large foil packet, leaving room for heat circulation inside.

GRILL 18 to 20 minutes in covered grill **OR BAKE** 30 to 35 minutes on a cookie sheet in oven. If desired, serve with sour cream.

Makes 4 to 6 servings

Prep Time: 15 minutes
Grill Time: 18 minutes

BLT Chicken Salad for Two

2 boneless skinless chicken breasts
¼ cup mayonnaise or salad dressing
½ teaspoon black pepper
4 large lettuce leaves
1 large tomato, seeded and diced
3 slices bacon, crisp-cooked and crumbled
1 hard-cooked egg, sliced
   Salad dressing (optional)

1. Prepare grill for direct cooking.

2. Brush chicken with mayonnaise; sprinkle with pepper. Grill over medium heat 5 to 7 minutes per side or until no longer pink in center. Cool slightly; cut into thin strips.

3. Arrange lettuce on serving plates. Top with chicken, tomato, bacon and egg. Serve with salad dressing. *Makes 2 servings*

Nine-Layer Salad

6 cups baby spinach, packed
1½ cups grape tomatoes
2 cups pattypan squash, halved crosswise
1 cup peas, blanched
4 ounces baby corn, halved lengthwise
2 cups baby carrots, blanched and halved lengthwise
1 cup peppercorn-ranch salad dressing
1 cup shredded Cheddar cheese
4 slices bacon, crisp-cooked and crumbled

1. Layer spinach, tomatoes, squash, peas, corn and carrots in 4-quart glass bowl. Pour dressing over salad; spread evenly. Top with cheese. Cover and refrigerate 4 hours.

2. Before serving, sprinkle with bacon. *Makes 7 servings*

New England Baked Beans

4 slices bacon, chopped

3 cans (about 15 ounces each) Great Northern beans, rinsed and drained

¾ cup water

1 small onion, chopped

⅓ cup canned diced tomatoes, well drained

3 tablespoons packed light brown sugar

3 tablespoons maple syrup

3 tablespoons molasses

2 cloves garlic, minced

½ teaspoon salt

½ teaspoon dry mustard

⅛ teaspoon black pepper

½ bay leaf

SLOW COOKER DIRECTIONS

1. Cook bacon in large skillet over medium-high heat until chewy but not crisp. Drain on paper towels. Combine bacon, beans, water, onion, tomatoes, brown sugar, maple syrup, molasses, garlic, salt, mustard, pepper and bay leaf in slow cooker.

2. Cover; cook on LOW 6 to 8 hours or until mixture is thickened. Remove bay leaf before serving. *Makes 4 to 6 servings*

BACON BITS

Cooking times are guidelines. Slow cookers, just like ovens, cook differently depending on heating units. You may need to slightly adjust cooking times for your slow cooker.

The publisher would like to thank the companies and organizations listed below for the use of their recipes and photographs in this publication.

Alouette® Spreadable Cheese

Campbell Soup Company

Dole Food Company, Inc.

The Hershey Company

Kraft Foods Global, Inc.

Reckitt Benckiser Inc.

Recipes courtesy of the Reynolds Kitchens

Sargento® Foods Inc.

Unilever

Wisconsin Milk Marketing Board

METRIC CONVERSION CHART

VOLUME MEASUREMENTS (dry)

$1/8$ teaspoon = 0.5 mL
$1/4$ teaspoon = 1 mL
$1/2$ teaspoon = 2 mL
$3/4$ teaspoon = 4 mL
1 teaspoon = 5 mL
1 tablespoon = 15 mL
2 tablespoons = 30 mL
$1/4$ cup = 60 mL
$1/3$ cup = 75 mL
$1/2$ cup = 125 mL
$2/3$ cup = 150 mL
$3/4$ cup = 175 mL
1 cup = 250 mL
2 cups = 1 pint = 500 mL
3 cups = 750 mL
4 cups = 1 quart = 1 L

VOLUME MEASUREMENTS (fluid)

1 fluid ounce (2 tablespoons) = 30 mL
4 fluid ounces ($1/2$ cup) = 125 mL
8 fluid ounces (1 cup) = 250 mL
12 fluid ounces ($1 1/2$ cups) = 375 mL
16 fluid ounces (2 cups) = 500 mL

WEIGHTS (mass)

$1/2$ ounce = 15 g
1 ounce = 30 g
3 ounces = 90 g
4 ounces = 120 g
8 ounces = 225 g
10 ounces = 285 g
12 ounces = 360 g
16 ounces = 1 pound = 450 g

DIMENSIONS

$1/16$ inch = 2 mm
$1/8$ inch = 3 mm
$1/4$ inch = 6 mm
$1/2$ inch = 1.5 cm
$3/4$ inch = 2 cm
1 inch = 2.5 cm

OVEN TEMPERATURES

250°F = 120°C
275°F = 140°C
300°F = 150°C
325°F = 160°C
350°F = 180°C
375°F = 190°C
400°F = 200°C
425°F = 220°C
450°F = 230°C

BAKING PAN SIZES

Utensil	Size in Inches/Quarts	Metric Volume	Size in Centimeters
Baking or Cake Pan (square or rectangular)	$8 \times 8 \times 2$	2 L	$20 \times 20 \times 5$
	$9 \times 9 \times 2$	2.5 L	$23 \times 23 \times 5$
	$12 \times 8 \times 2$	3 L	$30 \times 20 \times 5$
	$13 \times 9 \times 2$	3.5 L	$33 \times 23 \times 5$
Loaf Pan	$8 \times 4 \times 3$	1.5 L	$20 \times 10 \times 7$
	$9 \times 5 \times 3$	2 L	$23 \times 13 \times 7$
Round Layer Cake Pan	$8 \times 1 1/2$	1.2 L	20×4
	$9 \times 1 1/2$	1.5 L	23×4
Pie Plate	$8 \times 1 1/4$	750 mL	20×3
	$9 \times 1 1/4$	1 L	23×3
Baking Dish or Casserole	1 quart	1 L	—
	$1 1/2$ quart	1.5 L	—
	2 quart	2 L	—